Dancers

ANTHONY CRICKMAY

other books by Anthony Crickmay

LYNN SEYMOUR
THE PRINCIPLES OF CLASSICAL DANCE

DANCERS

Dancers

ANTHONY CRICKMAY

Introduction by
ANDREW PORTER

William Morrow and Company, Inc.

New York   1982

CRICKMAY

to

Dame Ninette de Valois

*There are many people who have given me help and advice,
and to mention only a few is ungrateful ; but without the constant
encouragement and steadfast friendship of Sheila and Andrew
Porter, Peter Williams, Mary Clarke, Clement Crisp, Eileen
Jezzi, Gale and Lenny Law, Jerry Penciss, John Higgins and
Bob Cohan the faltering moments would not have been passed by so
easily. Also my deep thanks to my Mother and sister June for all
they have done for me.*

A.C.

*Photographs no. 35, 36 and 58 are reproduced from Vogue.
© Conde Nast Publications Ltd. Photograph no. 57 is reproduced
from 'The Principles of Classical Dance' by Joan Lawson,
A & C Black Ltd, 1979.*

Copyright © 1982 by Anthony Crickmay
Introduction copyright © 1982 by Andrew Porter

First published in the United States of America in 1982 by
William Morrow and Company, Inc.

Library of Congress Catalog Card Number: 81-48551

ISBN: 0-688-01239-6

Printed in Great Britain

1 2 3 4 5 6 7 8 9 10

In their stillness Nijinsky's pictures have more vitality than the dances they remind us of as we now see them on the stage. They remain to show us what dancing can be : and what the spectator and the dancer each aspire to, and hold to be a fair standard of art. I think they give the discouraged dance lover faith in dancing as a serious human activity.

Edwin Denby: *Notes on Nijinsky Photographs (1943).*

Dance—images created by mind and muscle, moving through time, traced in air and on earth by human bodies—is the most fleeting of the arts. Not with pencil or paints, or in stone, or with notes whose pitches, durations, and timbres can be defined, or in words are those images given form. The medium is living bodies—dancers. A composer may write a role for a favourite soprano, and her art may not only inspire but in some ways even determine what he writes—or at least how he writes it. But, in customary dance parlance, a choreographer composes a leading role *on* his ballerina, and the choice of preposition reflects the fact that she is not only the interpreter of his ideas (and perhaps inspirer of some of them) but also the very material through which he makes those ideas manifest. Without living dancers to work on, most choreographers are like painters without paint and canvas—able to plan and dream of new works but not to execute them. Most choreographers, not all : there are some who can compose and complete a dance on paper or in the mind, and come to the company with every pattern shaped, each detail decided. But they are exceptions. Watching a dance being made is more often than not rather like studying the growth of a symphony through a composer's successive drafts, or the growth of a large canvas through an artist's preliminary sketches. With this difference : that the composer's and the artist's early sketches, set down, can be preserved, while the choreographer's first drafts, traced in the studio 'on' his living medium, disappear once they have been rejected, refined, or replaced. With other differences too : analogues between the arts must be handled with care. But the loose similes may help to suggest why dance is fleeting ; and why the images of great dance and great dancers which remain when human memories of the originals have faded are to be cherished.

Memory has remained the chief means of transmission. Dance notation has been developed to a point where it can plot positions in time with some accuracy, but hardly nuances or individual personality. (A recording can set down for posterity every inflexion of a great singer; no dance notation can yet set down the exact timing and inflexion in all its parts of a particular arabesque.) Films can be useful, but often—as Lincoln Kirstein has written of dance films—'while supposedly anatomizing movement, they leave no fixed impression or any synthesized wholeness'. Dances of the past can be reconstructed from a compound of notation, written descriptions, from earlier ages engravings, and from later ones films and photographs. Some ballets have been handed on from generation to generation, and altered in the process. The *Giselles* we see today are not the *Giselle* of 1841, although the original 'idea' and perhaps some of the original images survive. (Whereas Beethoven's Opus 131 in whatever modern reprint of the score remains the string quartet that Beethoven composed in 1826.) Reconstruction is a work for specialists. The most vivid testimony—as Edwin Denby suggests in the sentences cited above—is often to be found in the work of an outstanding dance photographer.

Photography is another art: an art of stillness, and one over whose results the artist exercises full, personal control. Although his lights, lenses, chemicals, and papers may sometimes seem to have taken on a life of their own, in fact he commands them as surely as a painter commands his pigments. (Of course, like any other creator, he may on occasion seize and claim some happy effect of chance.) Photography says to the passing moment 'Tarry awhile, thou art so fair'—or so fearsome, so telling, so lyrical. But dance photography of the kind found in these pages is not just the arresting for all time of a moment perceived—although among other things it is that. The pictures in this volume are, it seems to me, compositions. In common with choreography, they result from a collaboration between subject and creator, but here the subjects are not simultaneously the medium of expression. Anthony Crickmay's great-grandfather and grandfather were architects, whose sound—and occasionally exuberant—buildings stand in many parts of Dorset. (Thomas Hardy worked for a while in the Crickmay office.) There is something of the architect in their descendant; the structure and the careful balance of his photographs show it, and so does his quick response to 'architectural' moments in specific ballets. Sometimes he has functioned as his own choreographer, worked with dancers not to capture moments in an existing dance but to create pure images of the shapes, patterns, weights—or apparent weightlessness—that the body of a particular dancer can compass. The studies of Micha Bergese, for example, come from an 'abstract' series exploring line, muscles, and movement; those of Robert Solomon from a series exploring body shapes as a kind of kinetic sculpture. Elsewhere, Anthony Dowell and Crickmay join to celebrate the lyrical beauty of correct classical placing. But many of the photographs are photographs of record; and in discussing these I must 'declare an interest'.

For a dozen years or so, Anthony Crickmay and I chronicled dance together in the arts page of *The Financial Times*, he with images and I in words. His first dance photograph to be published—of Yury Soloviev at the high point of a character leap, as Danila, the stone-carver in the Grigorovich–Prokofiev *The Stone Flower*—appeared on June 20th, 1961, when the Kirov Ballet was at Covent Garden for the first time. My review tells of the young Soloviev's power, his magnificent leap, his directness, his lack of any affectation (for in those days Soloviev was a less mannered dancer than he later became). Crickmay's photograph shows it all, vividly, at a glance. It was the start of a long and happy collaboration. *The Financial Times* allowed space for large pictures and space for lengthy reviews. Its editor had allotted us, to deal with the daily assemblage of the page, a young man, John Higgins—now arts editor of *The Times*—with an eye and an enthusiasm for good pictures, a flair for displaying them to advantage even within the limitations of newspaper format, and a welcome exigence about block-making and typesetting. While they lasted, they were golden years for a critic; at high season, the three of us would be in almost daily discussion, planning, appraising, and proposing. Then Higgins went to *The Times*; I went to New York, and wrote about dance in a magazine that did not use photographs; Crickmay suffered, and finally broke with, 'arts editors' who viewed photographs as mere illustrations, something to 'break up the type'. But, of course, he continued to photograph dance. They were also golden years for dance. At Covent Garden, Frederick Ashton was creating his late masterpieces. Margot Fonteyn was still dancing. In *Marguerite et Armand*, Ashton composed an allegory of a mature, beautiful woman stirred to new intensity and passion by the arrival of a new partner; and Rudolf Nureyev's presence in the company spurred its male dancers to new achievement. Anthony Dowell emerged as their most elegant stylist. What Fonteyn was to Ashton, Lynn Seymour was to Kenneth MacMillan, and in *Anastasia* MacMillan displayed—and extended—Seymour's rare power and eloquence as a dramatic ballerina. Ballet Rambert moved from being a classical company into something more modern; Glen Tetley's works loomed large in its repertory, and Christopher Bruce was its star. Festival Ballet pursued its traditional course, and some of its higher points are recorded in these pages. Western Theatre Ballet moved north, to be re-established as Scottish Ballet. And all over the country smaller companies were dancing.

The Bolshoy and Kirov ballets, Netherlands Dance Theatre, and the Stuttgart ballet, with Marcia Haydée and Richard Cragun, were prominent among the many visiting troupes. (Meanwhile, as Crickmay's fame as a dance photographer grew, he was increasingly often summoned abroad—westward to Canada, eastward as far as Iran—to photograph dance there.) The visiting company that left the deepest, most lasting mark on British dance was Martha Graham's—not so much directly as because it inspired a handful of enthusiasts with the determination that Britain, too, should possess a school of modern dance ('school' in both senses of the word) disciplined, coherent, and firmly founded. The London School of Contemporary Dance and the London Contemporary Dance Company, established and for many years funded by Robin Howard, were the result. Robert Cohan, formerly a leading Graham dancer, then teacher, choreographer, shaper, and inspirer of the new company, played—and continues to play—the kind of role there that Ninette de Valois did for the Royal Ballet. The troupe, grounded in the Graham technique, soon developed a style, idiom, and character of its own. *Dancers* is not a formal picture-chronicle of dance in the last twenty years but, rather, a personal anthology of images drawn from them. Nevertheless, the picture of those decades which it presents is wide-ranging, and it is the first of general scope, I believe, which adequately reflects the London Contemporary Dance Company's place in the dance spectrum of today. The Graham company's visit to Britain in 1960 was also crucial to Crickmay's development as a dance photographer. It opened his eyes—as it did those of many others—to a new range of expressive imagery, new possibilities in dance. It inspired some of his most exciting pictures to that date, and it moved him to invent and develop new techniques in which to picture these new poses and movements.

Let me touch on that topic later. It is tempting to dwell a shade longer on this book as a record of two decades of dancing: a 'record' continuing with, among much else, *Mayerling*, the London Contemporary Dance Company's later work, the arrival in the West of Natalia Makarova and Mikhail Baryshnikov, and a new generation of British dancers. And inevitable, perhaps, for someone who saw most of the dances and dancers pictured herein; who, turning the pages, is suddenly arrested by Alla Sizova in *The Stone Flower*, Lynn Seymour in *Anastasia*, Mary Hinkson in *Circe*, Christopher Bruce in *Pierrot Lunaire*, and then stops to remember and relive those ballets. One of a dance photographer's high achievements is the ability to 'distil' the essence, or some essence, of a dance in a single image—choosing not necessarily the most obvious or most spectacular moment but one so timed, lit, composed, and then printed as to be most revelatory. Dancers say that Crickmay's shutter clicks on them at unexpected moments—which turn out to have been the right ones. But 'taking' the picture is only the first step; them comes making it. (Sparks have flown when an editor's insensitive cropping has altered the architecture of a Crickmay print, or bad block-making has spoiled its tonal proportions. Removing a strip from a uniform but carefully planned background, too dense—or insufficiently dense—a rendering of the surrounding space, can drain the life from a vivid picture, mute or muffle its statement.) In an early interview, which Crickmay now blushes to recall, he once tried to expound a 'philosophy' of dance photography and told of the rare, satisfying moments when some picture of his seemed to him to 'say' exactly what he thought and felt about some dance or dancer. He need not blush. If dance criticism, dance commentary, is a response at once analytic and poetic to those moving images in space, then Crickmay is one of our most perceptive, precise and appreciative critics. I'd qualify that only by adding that Crickmay as revealed in this book may seem on occasion too generous a critic. There are perhaps a few pages here—I shan't suggest which—that make some dancers and some ballets seem rather better, I think, than they really were.

The observation, however, serves as a reminder that commentary or criticism is only one aspect of the collection, and not the most important. The 'bad takes'—with wrong notes or cracked notes—of a soprano in the recording studio are not preserved; what gets published is her achievement at its highest. And I have seen Crickmay photographs—brilliant photographs—that devastatingly expose faulty technique or feeble invention. They plainly have no place in such an anthology as this, which is at once a personal record of dance enjoyed through two decades by one who saw a great deal of it; an enthusiast's appreciation; and also, by any reckoning, a collection of remarkable photographs. A person blind to dance in all its aspects could hardly miss the level of the photography. But the more someone cares about dance, the more he is likely to admire this sharp-eyed, sensitive, inventive response to it. The range of dance covered with understanding is astonishingly wide; so is the range of photographic techniques, developed and refined over the years. Some photographs are of performances in the theatre, others are composed in the studio. Some include décor, others have plain backgrounds. Some are of ensembles, and more are of individuals. Speed, lighting, contrasts of hard and soft, accents, and 'atmosphere' are matched to—or suggested by—the subjects. Crickmay has the true dance photographer's gift that Kirstein described as 'suggesting previous and subsequent action'; but there are also some memorable images of stillness. Perhaps above all, there is particularity: loving portrayal of the special qualities that make one great dancer different from another, the way an individual body moves, works, and 'sings'.

When, say fifty years hence, people ask what dance and dancers were like from 1960 to 1980, this book will do much to answer them. And beyond the dazzling, fastidious technical achievement there seems to lie the lyrical, impassioned statement of a belief: in the importance of the art Crickmay practices and of the art he loves and pictures.

ANDREW PORTER

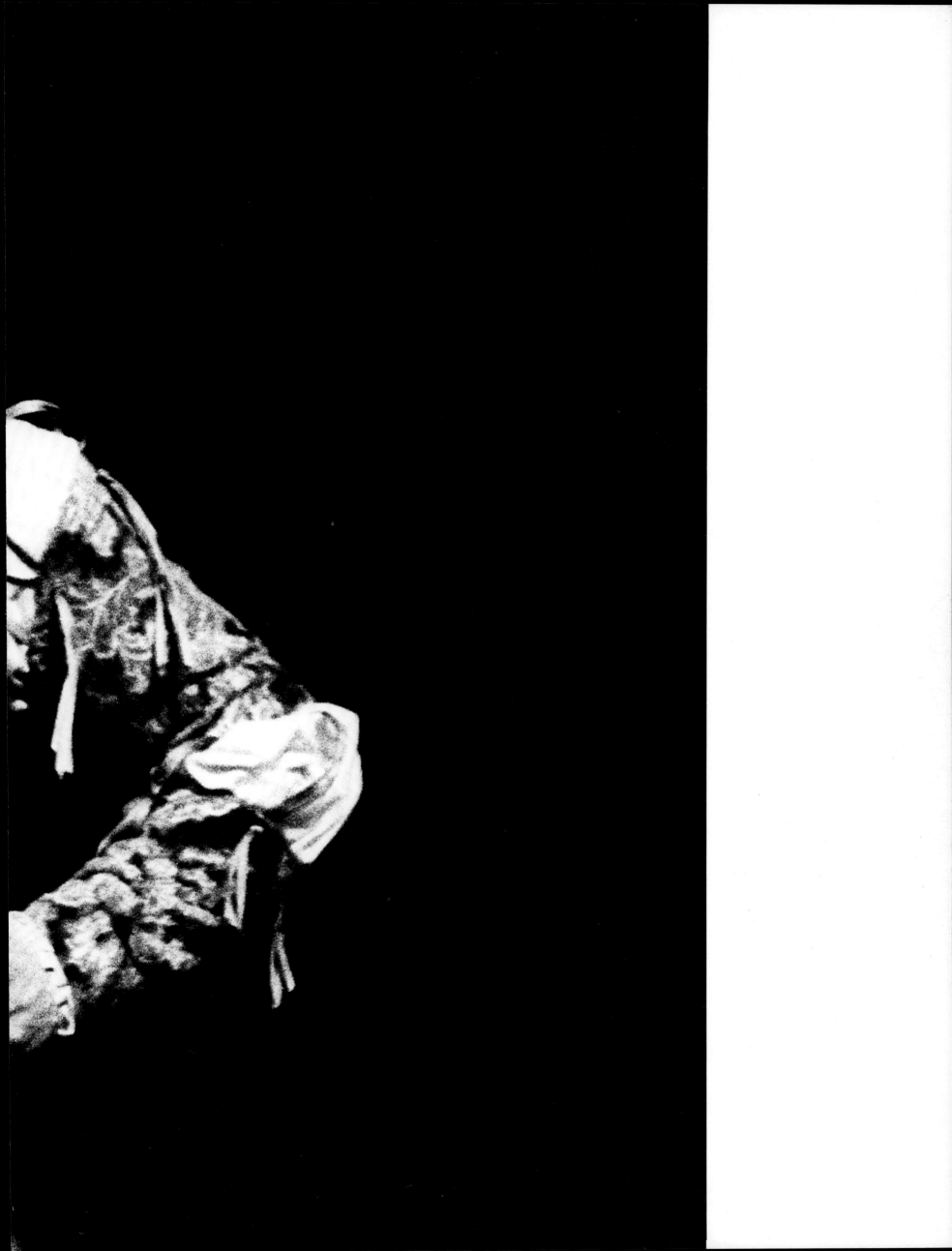

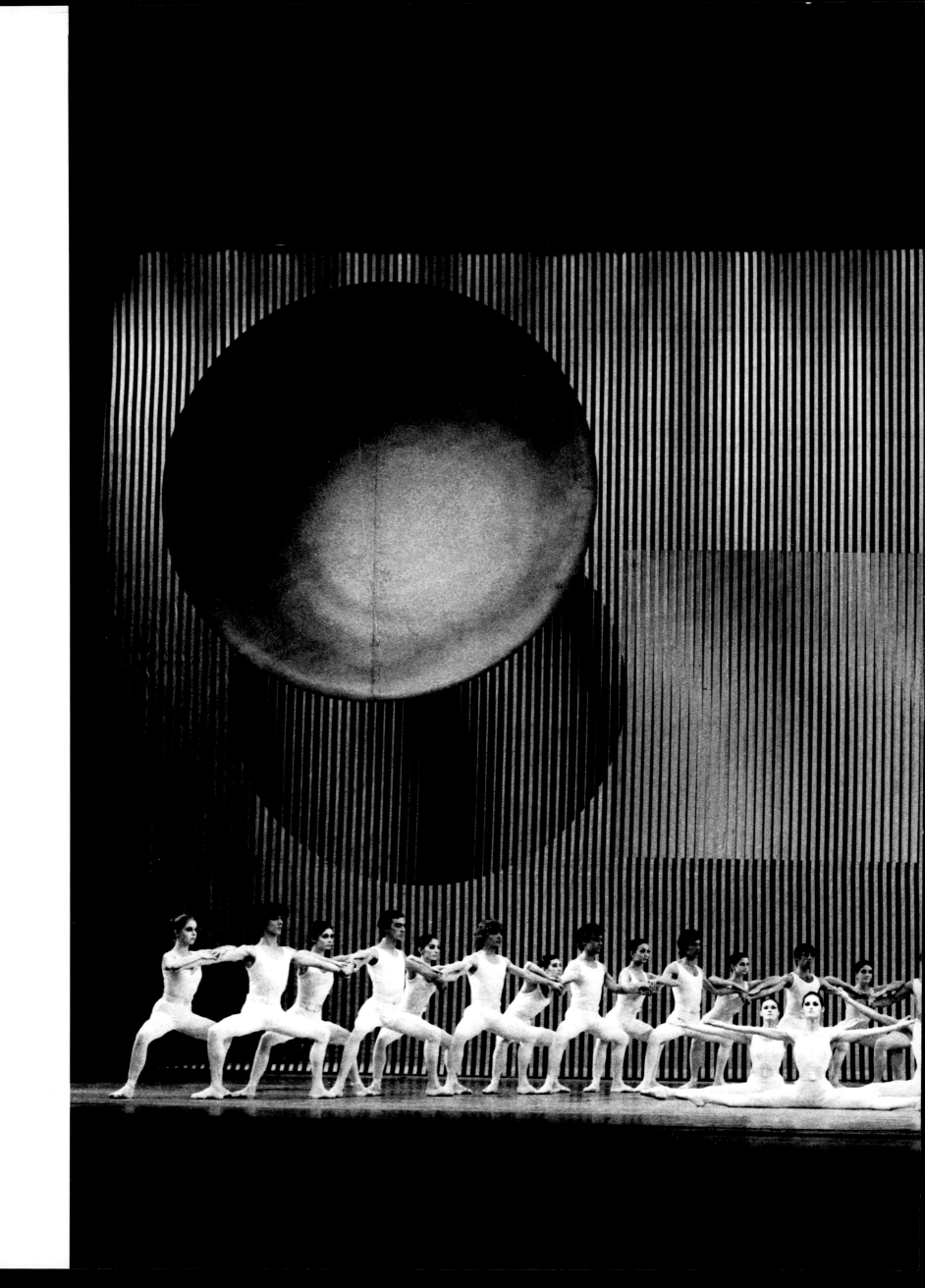

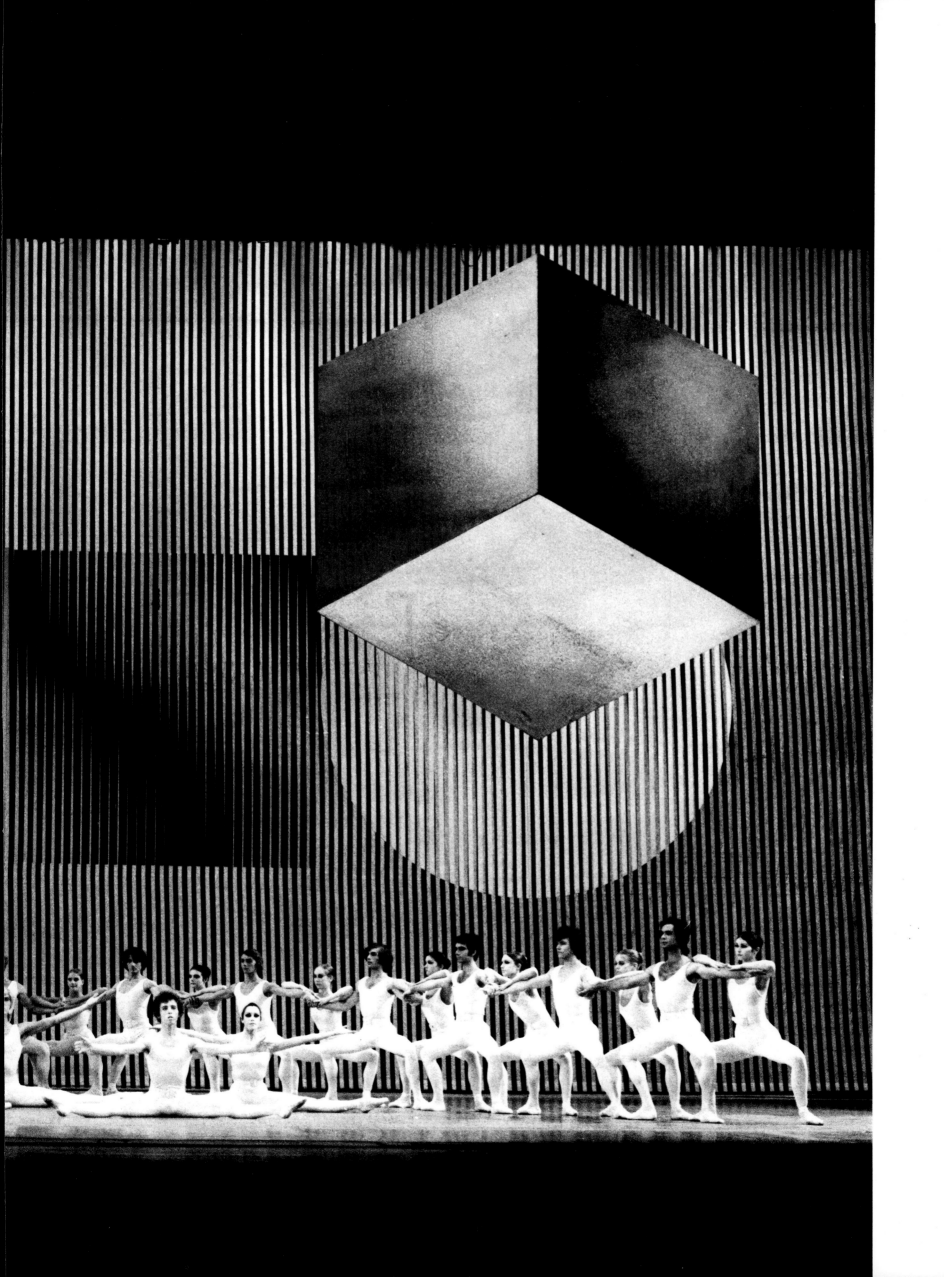

Index to the photographs

1 Dancer: Jane Landon
 Company: Royal Ballet
 Work: *Swan Lake*
 Choreographer: Petipa Ivanov, after N. Sergueyev
  with additional choreography by
  Frederick Ashton, revised by Ninette de Valois
 Designer: Leslie Hurry
 Music: Tchaikovsky
 Date of photograph: 7 June 1965

2 Dancers: Corps de Ballet
 Company: London Festival Ballet
 Work: *Conservatoire*
 Choreographer: A. Bournonville/M. Vangsaa
 Designer: M. Stennet
 Music: H. S. Pauli
 Date of photograph: 10 May 1974

3 Dancer: Rudolf Nureyev
 Company: London Festival Ballet
 Work: *Scheherezade*
 Date of photograph: 13 May 1978

4 Dancer: Elisabetta Terabust
 Company: London Festival Ballet
 Work: *Swan Lake*
 Choreographer: Beryl Grey after Petipa Ivanov,
  based on the version by N. Sergueyev
 Designer: Truscott
 Music: Tchaikovsky
 Date of photograph: 7 September 1977

5 Dancer: John Jones
 Company: Ballets U.S.A.
 Work: *Afternoon of a Faun*
 Choreographer: Jerome Robbins
 Designer (costumes): Irene Sharaff
 Music: Debussy
 Date of photograph: May 1961

6 Dancer: John Jones
 Company: Ballets U.S.A.
 Work: *Afternoon of a Faun*
 Choreographer: Jerome Robbins
 Date of photograph: May 1961

7 Dancer: Anthony Dowell in the studio
 Company: Royal Ballet
 Date of photograph: 11 April 1974

8 Dancer: Anthony Dowell in the studio
 Company: Royal Ballet
 Date of photograph: 11 April 1974

9 Dancers: Patrick Harding-Irmer
  and Anca Frankenhauser
 Company: London Contemporary Dance Theatre
 Work: *Forest*
 Choreographer: Robert Cohan
 Designer: Norberto Chiesa
 Music: Brian Hodgson
 Date of photograph: 9 December 1977

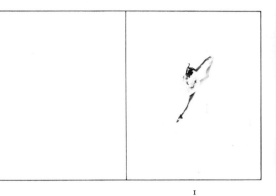

1

2

3 4

5 6

7 8

9

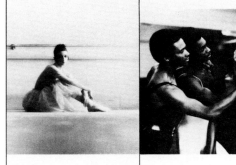

10   11   12   13   14

17   18   19   20   21

24   25   26   27   28   29

31   32   33   34   35   36

15   16

22   23

30

37   38

10   Dancer: Marcia Haydée in the rehearsal room
Company: Stuttgart Ballet
Date of photograph: 13 May 1974

11   Dancers: Arthur Mitchell, director of the Dance
Theatre of Harlem, rehearsing Ronald Perry
and Lydia Abarca in the studio
Date of photograph: 25 June 1974

12   Dancers: Margot Fonteyn and Frederick Ashton
at the Friends of Covent Garden Christmas party
Work: *Tonight at 8.30*
Music (arrangement): Peter Grenwell
Date of photograph: 16 December 1973

13   Dancer: Michael Coleman
Company: Royal Ballet
Work: *The Concert*
Choreographer: Jerome Robbins
Designer (scenery and lights); Jean Rosenthal;
(costumes): Irene Sharoff
Music: Chopin orchestrated by Clare Grundeman
Date of photograph: 5 March 1975

14   Dancer: Mikhail Baryshnikov
Company: Royal Ballet
Work: *Romeo and Juliet*
Choreographer: Kenneth MacMillan
Designer: Nicholas Georgiadis
Music: Prokofiev
Date of photograph: 21 October 1975

15   Dancers: Lynn Seymour and Anthony Dowell
Company: Royal Ballet
Work: *Voluntaries* (rehearsal)
Choreographer: Glen Tetley
Designer: Ruben Ter-Arutunian
Music: Poulenc (Concerto for Organ and Strings
and Timpani)
Date of photograph: 18 October 1976

16   Dancer: Jonathan Taylor
Company: Ballet Rambert
Work: *Time Base*
Date of photograph: 25 November 1966

17   Dancer: David Lamb in the studio
Date of photograph: 16 December 1979

18   Dancers: Margot Fonteyn and Rudolf Nureyev
Company: Royal Ballet
Work: *Marguerite and Armand*
Choreographer: Frederick Ashton
Designer: Cecil Beaton
Music: Liszt arranged by H. Searle
Date of photograph: 8 March 1963

19   Dancers: Marcia Haydée and Richard Cragun
in the studio
Company: Stuttgart Ballet
Date of photograph: 13 May 1974

20   Dancer: Marcia Haydée doing a barre in the studio
Company: Stuttgart Ballet
Date of photographer: 13 May 1974

21   Dancer: Jennifer Penney
Company: Royal Ballet
Work: *Swan Lake*
Choreographer: Petipa Ivanov after N. Sergueyev,
choreography by Frederick Ashton,
revised by Ninette de Valois
Music: Leslie Hurry
Date of photograph: 3 December 1979

22   Dancers: Margot Fonteyn and Rudolf Nureyev
Company: Royal Ballet
Work: *Don Juan*
Date of photograph: 24 January 1973

23   Dancer: Rudolf Nureyev
Company: Royal Ballet
Work: *The Prodigal Son*
Choreographer: George Balanchine
Designer: Roualt
Music: Prokofiev
Date of photograph: 24 January 1973

24   Dancer: Robert Solomon in the studio
Date of photograph: 25 November 1972

25   Dancer: Robert Solomon in the studio
Date of photograph: 25 November 1972

26   Dancer: Galina Samsova
Company: London Festival Ballet
Work: *Le Corsair*
Choreographer: Klavin, after Saint-Leon
Designer: P. Farmer
Music: Drigo
Date of photograph: 30 May 1971

27   Dancers: David Ashmole, Glen Tetley and
Lynn Seymour in rehearsal
Company: Royal Ballet
Work: *Voluntaries*
Choreographer: Glen Tetley
Date of photograph: 19 June 1976

28   Dancers: Marilyn Rowe and John Meehan
Company: Australian Ballet
Work: *Gemini*
Choreographer: Glen Tetley
Designer: Nadine Baylis
Music: H. W. Henze (Symphony No. 3)
Date of photograph: 8 October 1973

29   Dancer: Mary Hinkson
Company: Martha Graham Dance Company
Work: *Circe*
Choreographer: Martha Graham
Designer: I. Noguchi
Music: Hovhanes
Date of photograph: 13 September 1963

30   Dancer: Elisabetta Terabust
Company: London Festival Ballet
Work: *La Chatte*
Choreographer: Ronald Hynd
Designer: Peter Docherty
Music: Henri Sauget
Date of photograph: 22 June 1978

31   Dancers: Frank Polak and Soren Backlund
Company: Nederlands Dans Theater
Work: *Mythical Hunters*
Choreographer: Glen Tetley
Designer (costumes): Anthony Binstead
Music: Oedoen Partos
Date of photograph: 8 March 1968

32   Dancer: Mikhail Baryshnikov
Company: Royal Ballet
Work: *Romeo and Juliet*
Choreographer: Kenneth MacMillan
Designer: Nicholas Georgiadis
Music: Prokofiev
Date of photograph: 3 November 1975

33   Dancer: Martha Graham
Company: Martha Graham Dance Company
Work: *Clytemnestra*
Choreographer: Martha Graham
Designer: I. Noguchi; costumes: Martha Graham
Music: Halim El Dabh
Date of photograph: 25 August 1963

34   Dancer: Martha Graham
Company: Martha Graham Dance Company
Work: *Clytemnestra*
Choreographer: Martha Graham
Designer: I. Noguchi
Music: Halim El Dabh
Date of photograph: 5 September 1963

35   Dancer: Peter Schaufuss
Company: London Festival Ballet
Work: *Le Corsair*
Choreographer: after Saint-Léon
Designer: P. Farmer
Music: Drigo
Date of photograph: 1980

36   Dancer: Peter Schaufuss
Company: London Festival Ballet
Work: *Le Corsair*
Choreographer: after Saint-Léon
Designer: P. Farmer
Music: Drigo
Date of photograph: 1980

37   Dancer: Jennifer Penney
Company: Royal Ballet
Work: *The Sleeping Beauty*
Choreographer: Petipa, after N. Sergueyev, with
additional choreography by Frederick Ashton,
supervised by Ninette de Valois
Designer: David Walker
Music: Tchaikovsky
Date of photograph: 14 December 1966

38   Dancers: Natalia Makarova and Donald MacLeary
Company: Royal Ballet
Work: *Swan Lake*
Choreographer: Petipa/Ivanov after N. Sergueyev,
with additional choreography by Frederick Ashton,
revised by Ninette de Valois
Music: Tchaikovsky
Date of photograph: 26 June 1972

39   40   41   42   43

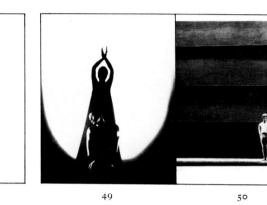

46   47   48   49   50

52   53   54   55   56

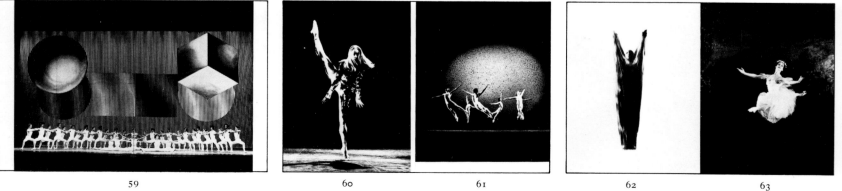

59   60   61   62   63

44   45

51

57   58

64   65

39 Dancers: Marcia Haydée and Richard Cragun
rehearsing with Glen Tetley in Stuttgart
Company: Stuttgart Ballet
Choreographer: Glen Tetley
Music: Poulenc
Date of photograph: 13 May 1973

40 Dancers: Linda Gibbs and Micha Bergese in the
studio
Company: London Contemporary Dance Theatre
Date of photograph: 24 June 1975

41 Dancer: Roland Price, winner of the Gold Medal
of the Royal Academy of Dancing, and
of the Adeleine Genee Medal, 1978, in the studio
Date of photograph: 4 February 1978

42 Dancer: Mikhail Baryshnikov in rehearsal
Company: Royal Ballet
Work: *Romeo and Juliet*
Choreographer: Kenneth MacMillan
Designer: Nicholas Georgiadis
Music: Prokofiev
Date of photograph: 8 October 1975

43 Dancer: Christopher Bruce in the studio
Company: Ballet Rambert
Date of photograph: 9 March 1976

44 Dancer: Natalia Makarova
Company: Royal Ballet
Work: *Manon*
Choreographer: Kenneth MacMillan
Designer: Nicholas Georgiadis
Music: Massenet
Date of photograph: 18 November 1974

45 Dancer: Margot Fonteyn in class,
at the Royal Ballet School Studios
Date of photograph: 1964

46 Dancers: Vyvyan Lorrayne
Company: Royal Ballet
Work: *Allegro Brillante*
Choreographer: George Balanchine
Designer: Karinska
Music: Tchaikovsky
Date of photograph: 2 March 1973

47 Dancers: Sandra Craig, Jonathan Taylor,
Christopher Bruce
Company: Ballet Rambert
Work: *Blind Sight*
Choreographer: Norman Morrice
Designer: Nadine Baylis
Music: Bob Downes
Date of photograph: 27 October 1969

48 Dancer: Lynn Seymour
Company: Royal Ballet
Work: *Isadora: A Tribute to Isadora Duncan*
Choreographer: Frederick Ashton
Date of photograph: 5 January 1976

49 Dancer: William Louther
Company: Contemporary Dance Company
Work: *Kontakion*
Date of photograph: 4 January 1972

50 Dancer: Anthony Dowell
Company: Royal Ballet
Work: *Four Schumann Pieces*
Choreographer: Hans Van Manen
Designer: Jean-Paul Vroom
Music: Schumann (Quartet in A Major Op. 41.
No. 3)
Date of photograph: 30 January 1975

51 Dancers l. to r.: Robert North, Tom Jobe, Siobhan
Davies, Kate Harrison, Charlotte Kirkpatrick,
Namron, Cathy Lewis, Paula Lansley, Anca
Frankenhauser, Anita Griffin, Anthony van Laast,
Christopher Bannerman, Charlotte Milner,
Micha Bergese, Sallie Estep, Philippe Giraudeau,
Celia Hulton
Company: London Contemporary Dance Theatre
Date of photograph: 17 March 1977

52 Dancer: Spanish dancer, Antonio, in the studio
Date of photograph: 1 November 1961

53 Dancer: Micha Bergese in the studio
Company: London Contemporary Dance Theatre
Date of photograph: 21 May 1972

54 Dancer: Frederick Ashton
Company: Royal Ballet
Work: *Cinderella*
Choreographer: Frederick Ashton
Designer: Bardon and Walker, after Malclès
Music: Prokofiev
Date of photograph: 22 December 1965

55 Dancers: Margot Fonteyn and Rudolf Nureyev
Company: Royal Ballet
Work: *Giselle*
Choreographer: Petipa, after Coralli and Perrot,
with additional choreography by Frederick Ashton
Designer: James Bailey
Music: Adolphe Adam
Date of photograph: 22 October 1964

56 Dancers: Gerard Lemaitre and Anja Licher
Company: Nederlands Dans Theater
Work: *Mutations*
Choreography: Glen Tetley
Designer: Nadine Baylis
Date of photograph: 16 July 1970

57 Dancer: Anthony Dowell in the studio
Date of photograph: 21 January 1978

58 Dancer: George de la Peña, rehearsing
in the studio for the movie, *Nijinsky*
Date of photograph: 13 December 1978

59 Company: National Ballet of Canada
Work: *Kraanerg*
Choreographer: Roland Petit
Designer: Victor Vasarely
Music: Jannis Xenakis
Date of photograph: 7 August 1971

60 Dancer: Lenny Westerdijk
Company: Nederlands Dans Theater
Work: *Dreams*
Choreographer: Anna Sokolow
Music: Bach/Webern/Teo Macero
Date of photograph: 24 August 1967

61 Company: Royal Ballet
Work: *Voluntaries*
Choreographer: Glen Tetley
Designer: Ruben Ter-Arutunian
Music: Poulenc (Concerto for Organ
and Strings and Timpani)
Date of photograph: 17 November 1976

62 Dancer: Carolyn Carlson in the studio
Date of photograph: 3 May 1973

63 Dancer: Marian St. Claire
Company: Scottish Ballet
Work: *La Sylphide*
Designer: Peter Cazalet
Date of photograph: 17 November 1973

64 Dancer: Stella Mae
Company: Emma Dance Company
Work: *Doin A (folk song)*
Choreographer: Royston Maldoom
Designer: Eilsa Berg/Graham Bowers
Music: Cheorghe Zamfir (Flute de Pan et Orgue
Vol. 3)
Date of photograph: 1 June 1977

65 Dancers: Patricia Ruanne and Paul Clarke
Company: London Festival Ballet
Work: *Prodigal Son (in ragtime)*
Choreographer: Barry Moreland
Designer: Michael Annals
Music: Scott Joplin and others, arranged
and orchestrated by Grant Hossak
Date of photograph: 7 May 1974

66

67

68

69

70

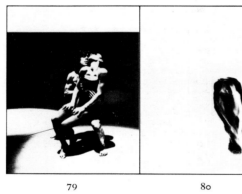

73

74

75

76

79

80

81

82

83

85

86

87

88

89